DETERMINED AND DANGEROUS

DETERMINED AND
DANGEROUS

FOR DRIVEN WOMEN STRIVING FOR MORE

DREAM BIG, ACCEPT NOTHING LESS AND DO WHAT IT
TAKES TO CREATE YOUR DREAM LIFE.

CHLOË BISSON

DETERMINED AND DANGEROUS
FOR DRIVEN WOMEN STRIVING FOR MORE

ISBN: 9781073543830 Paperback

This book also comes with a complimentary toolkit that guides you through how to overcome your challenges, channel your inner strength and start your own online business. Get your free toolkit here: www.determinedanddangerous.com/toolkit

DEDICATION

To women who have struggled in silence in the past and to those who are facing challenges right now. This is dedicated to you.

ACKNOWLEDGEMENTS

I wanted to start by giving special thanks to my Aunty Fran. Without her, I would never have overcome my biggest hurdle and I wouldn't have stumbled into this incredible venture.

I wanted to also thank my Mum. From a young age she showed me what it truly means to be an unstoppable woman. Without her I wouldn't know the importance of pushing myself to constantly grow and achieve more.

I wanted to also thank my Dad for being there when I need him the most. No matter how determined I get, I will always be his little girl at heart.

Finally, I wanted to thank Cedric, my incredible partner in crime. Without him, I wouldn't have had the idea to start my own business and I wouldn't have made it through the ups and downs. I wouldn't be where I am today.

INTRODUCTION

Life isn't like a box of chocolates. Life isn't even like riding a wave. It's like sitting on a rollercoaster that changes direction with no notice.

Waiting patiently as it slowly creeps up the incline and then, before you know it, it comes flying down spiraling you into the unknown.

Feeling sick with nerves whilst adrenaline is soaring around your body and when you think it's finished, it takes you around the circuit again.

Well, that's exactly what it felt like to me.

I was living the "perfect life", or so I thought at the time. I had an amazing job, I had a great boyfriend and I had a beautiful new home that we'd just bought together.

But then everything changed.

I lost my job, I lost my relationship, I lost my home and I was diagnosed with severe clinical depression. I watched as my dream life slipped through my fingers.

But that was only the start of my journey. That wasn't the ending, it was the beginning.

Since then I've overcome my depression, started my own business and learnt how to use my challenges to fuel me and give me the determination to reach even higher.

I've spent years journaling my story, all of the ups and the downs, because from the minute I overcame my depression I knew I wanted to share my journey so it would help others in the future.

And that's exactly what this book is all about.

It's about learning the strategies that I used to help you to deal with the whiplash of life, find your inner strength and learn how to use your challenges to fuel you.

The thing is, there isn't one particular moment when my determination was born.

It was a combination of everything. The break ups, the depression, the challenges, the successes, all of these experiences gave birth to my determination.

This is what has shown me the path to be *Determined and Dangerous* and this is exactly what I want to share with you.

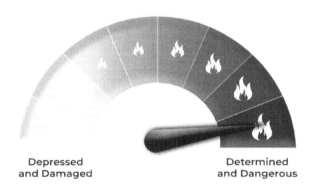

Depressed
and Damaged

Determined
and Dangerous

SECTION ONE

WHERE IT ALL BEGAN

"I trust that everything happens for a reason, even if we are not wise enough to see it."

— Oprah Winfrey

1

THE DAY EVERYTHING CHANGED

It was a Sunday. I woke up with makeup all over my pillow and my head was pounding.

We'd had a Halloween party at our new house the night before and a few friends came over to celebrate with us.

I was so thirsty and all I could feel was my throbbing headache. I couldn't even lift my head off the pillow but my phone kept dinging.

I looked at my phone, thinking the dinging was messages coming in from the girls sharing stories of last night, but instead I had a message from some random guy, Shane*.

"Hi Chloë, it's Shane. I'm so sorry to be the one to tell you this but I think you have a right to know. Dean has been sleeping with Nina."

I can't remember the exact words of the message and I remember it being a lot longer but you get the gist.

Dean* was my boyfriend of the past 5 years. We'd been together since we were 18 and we had just bought a 4 bedroom house together. We'd had our ups and downs like every young relationship does but nothing prepared me for what was about to come.

Nina* was my best friend's sister. I knew she had been treated badly in relationships before but I never expected this.

*Let's be honest - Dean and Nina are not their real names but I'm not going to name and shame and you'll find out why later.

Suddenly the pounding of my headache had gone and all I could feel was my heart racing like crazy.

I felt sick.

"No this can't be true, he wouldn't do that to me."

I felt confused.

"But what if he did?

Should I ask him?"

Then I felt guilty.

"No I can't ask him.

If he didn't do it he'll never forgive me for doubting him.

I'm just going to have to ask otherwise I'll never know"

I went downstairs and asked him one simple question:

"I've just had a really strange message from Shane, do you have something to tell me?"

The next thing that came out of his mouth told me everything I needed to know...

"Yes I do"

That's when my world collapsed.

He didn't tell me everything but he told me what I needed to hear.

He told me that it was a huge mistake and that I meant the world to him.

He told me that he would do anything to be with me.

But I knew that we would never be able to make it back.

The lies had gone too far and that's where our relationship ended.

That's the moment that everything changed.

I moved out of our new four bedroom house as I couldn't bear being in the home we'd bought together, where I'd dreamt of our future together.

So, I moved back in with my Mum and Step-Dad.

I couldn't eat.

I couldn't sleep.

I couldn't even talk to one of my closest friends about it because it was her sister.

I couldn't do anything except cry.

I felt like my world had collapsed.

Little did I know it was about to get so much worse.

2

THE OLD ME

So, I've always been a pretty determined person and I've always loved situations when there is the opportunity to achieve the unexpected.

I was brought up in the little island of Jersey in the Channel Islands, which is renowned for being full of wealthy families but my family wasn't one of them.

My parents split up when I was 10 years old and that's the first time I can remember feeling overwhelmed with determination. I absolutely loved both of my parents but together they had stalled and, as an only child, it wasn't fair on them to stay together just for me.

My parents worked hard so that they could afford to send me to a private all-girls school and, even though not being one of the "rich kids" didn't really bother me, I was determined to succeed and show my parents that it was worth every penny.

It was assumed that everyone attending the school would be going to university (I mean why wouldn't they!) but I couldn't justify my parents spending that amount of money just because I thought I had to follow the "norm".

So, instead, I took a leap of faith and went straight to work at the age of 18. Even though I felt so out of place and so behind, I knew I had to keep going to succeed.

I met Dean a few weeks after I started my first job and it was perfect timing. We had both just left school and started new chapters of our lives so it felt right.

Flash-forward three years, I went from feeling like the runt of the litter in a big four accountancy firm to being top of the class and qualifying as a Chartered Certified Accountant by the age of 21.

I saved every penny I could to buy my first property, and then three years into our relationship, Dean and I bought a beautiful four bedroom house together and it felt like everything was falling into place.

I felt like all of the challenges I'd faced so far were in the past and this was the time when I could take my foot off the accelerator and enjoy the rest of the ride.
I couldn't have been more wrong.

3

A CONVERSATION WITH MYSELF – PART 1

Then me: "Everything I've known has been a lie. How could he do this to me?!"

Now me: "He didn't do it to you, he did it to him. It wasn't about you, it was about what he needed at the time. I know it's hard but you will get through this – I promise."

Then me: "But what did I do to deserve this?"

Now me: "You didn't do anything to deserve this. It just happened. I know it hurts but you can't blame yourself for his actions."

Then me: "But what if I never feel myself again?"

Now me: "He didn't make you who you are, you did. You are still yourself now, you're just a different version of yourself – You've got this."

Then me: "But what if I can't be happy without him?"

Now me: "But what if you can be even happier?"

4

CONTROL

One of the most common emotions when dealing with a break up is the sudden urge or need to be in control of your life again. We feel the need to prove that we are not vulnerable or helpless and that we have our sh*t together.

This was something I personally experienced a lot.

I mean, I'd always been a bit of a control freak but now I was like a control freak on steroids, figuratively speaking.

The truth is though, we don't actually need to be in control all of the time. What we really seek is a *sense* of control.

The sense of control is broken down into two core parts; power and trust. You can get a sense of control by taking control and acting, which is effectively about power.

On the other hand, you can feel the sudden need for control when your trust has been broken.

That's exactly what happened to me.

Before that night, I felt completely in control of my life. I had a great job, I had a boyfriend that loved me and I had a beautiful new home. But then out of nowhere, I felt like I had lost every element of control in my life.

I felt like I could trust no one.

I felt like I had no power.

I felt helpless.

So, after the weeks of crying and feeling sorry for myself, the first real emotion I felt was the need to take control again.

Get back my strength.

Get back my power.

Get back my determination.

So that's exactly what I did.

I considered all areas of my life and asked myself one simple question:

"Which parts of my life am I in control of right?"

Within My Control:

- **Career** – *Working 50 hours a week never hurt anyone, right?*
- **Finances** – *If you don't count the four bedroom house I bought that I now can't live in, yeah sure!*
- **Physical Health** – *The gym is my sanctuary!*
- **Family** – *Thank god for my Mum's spare room…*

Out of My Control:

- **Relationships** – *Obviously Not!*
- **Friends** – *Not Anymore…*
- **Social** – *Who Needs A Social Life Anyway…*
- **Mental Health** – *Does Controlling When I'm Crying Count?*

In all seriousness though, it wasn't a surprise that half of those areas I felt I had little to no control over at that point in my life.

The break up affected my mental health a lot, specifically my self-esteem.

It affected my friendships because Nina was quite close to a number of my close friends which caused a bit of awkwardness amongst us, not to mention Dean being part of that same friendship group.

This caused an impact on my social life as I felt like I didn't want to go out and be seen in public in fear of seeing either of them or seeing others that would look at me like I was broken.

So, I looked at those four areas as a to-do list and started from the top.

Was I feeling like I was out of control because I had no power over whether or not I would see them if I left the house?

Or was I feeling like I was out of control because if I did see them, I couldn't trust myself to keep my mouth shut?

It was very clear that all of the control issues stemmed from the break up and I just needed to take the first step to dealing with those issues in order to start getting my life back.

5

THE FIRST STEP OUTSIDE

I've never done anything by halves. When I decided I was going to start taking back control of my situation I took the bull by the horns and did it all in one go.

I dealt with the relationship with my ex, the awkwardness with our friends and overcame my fear of my social life all in one night.

Our group of friends were all going out for someone's birthday, looking back I can't remember whose it was, all I can remember is how sick I felt knowing I had to go.

It was my first night out in public after the whole thing and I knew everyone would be on edge waiting to see how we would be around each other.

I decided I wasn't going to let his stupid mistake define the rest of my life, especially the time I had with my friends.

So, I spoke to him and gave him clear instructions. After all, he owed me. He couldn't exactly say no.

I can't remember the full conversation, other than my specific request:

"We're both going out tonight and I don't want it to be awkward. If you have as much respect for me as you say you do then I want you to do something."

I think he was a little nervous as to what I was going to say. Not to mention the fact that I was clearly fighting the urge to punch him in the face but I'm sure that wasn't *that* obvious…

"As soon we're both there, no matter who arrives first, you're going to come up to me, say hi, give me a hug and have a drink with me."

He might have been in shock but he shrugged his shoulders and agreed.

The night came, he walked in and everyone looked at me to see my reaction but he did exactly what I had asked.

The tension was suddenly gone.

You could literally feel the sigh in the air as we had a drink together.

It was one of the hardest things I've ever done, having to put on a brave face and act as if everything was ok, but it was what I had to do, not just for me but for our friends.

There was no way I was going to let this situation affect our friendship group any longer. There was no way I was going to miss out anymore because of something that I had had no control of.

I was done feeling sorry for myself.

6

FORGIVENESS

The break up with Dean was one of the most painful experiences of my life, or so I thought at the time. It went on for years due to how connected our lives were, owning property together and sharing the same group of friends, but I'll spare you the years of ups and downs!

I pushed myself into my work and I was more determined than ever - I was pushing for the next promotion, moved to one of our other offices - I kept telling myself life was good.

I was offered my dream job, amazing money, incredible experience and so much potential. Chloë Bisson, Director of a global fund manager. I gave my business cards out to everyone and anyone. Becoming a Director at 24 years old was and is still one of my proudest achievements.

But I realised that I was still holding onto a lot of my hate and resentment towards the situation with Dean and Nina.

I realised there was one thing left to truly let go of that had happened to me.

You see, whilst I was still dealing with the betrayal and pain caused by Dean, I was still civil to him and it wouldn't bother me if I saw him with our friends. But with Nina, it was a whole different story. It was like every time I saw her it was a reminder of everything.

We would be having a girl's night out and suddenly she would walk in and the whole environment would change. Everyone felt awkward, her sister would go over to her and say hi and the rest of our friends would look awkwardly at me to know whether they should stay with me or go and say hi too. I never once told them they couldn't talk to her but the tension between us didn't make the situation any easier.

Maybe I felt more betrayed by her because I'd known her longer or I'd been there for her in the past, who knows. But the truth was she didn't do anything worse than Dean and I realised that by holding onto this resentment, I was actually only hurting myself.

I knew it was time to forgive her too.

At first, I forgave her more for me than for anyone else as I knew I was only hurting myself by holding onto the resentment, but when I actually forgave her I realised how much it had been hurting her too.

So, after a year of not talking to her I turned up at her front door.

At the time my best friend (and her sister) was actually living with her. When she answered the door she looked shocked and mumbled under her breath that her sister wasn't home.

"It's okay. I'm here to see you."

To this day I don't know what was going through her mind at the time but all I could see was her nerves as she opened the door and let me in.

I explained to her that I thought it was time to move on, that we'd never be best friends but it had gone on long enough and it was time to forgive and forget.

I can't remember what we talked about after that. All I can remember was the relief on her face and the weight being lifted between us.

I think her sister was in just as much shock when she came home to find us sat in her living room catching up over a cup of tea.

That was the day when I finally felt like I had let go of everything that had happened.

Flash forward a few years, Dean started dating a girl I knew through a friend. I was actually really glad he was happy and they seemed like the perfect match. Don't get me wrong, there were a few jokes shared like "Make sure you keep it in your pants this time" and so on, but as if he could get away with it that easily.

Nina met a guy who treated her like a princess, finally she found a good guy! They went on to have two beautiful children together and got engaged. Would you believe I actually went to her hen party?!

I grew a lot as a person over those few years, more than the last few pages can even summarise.

We'd all moved on from the situation and I had forgiven Dean and Nina.

So why did I still feel so damaged?

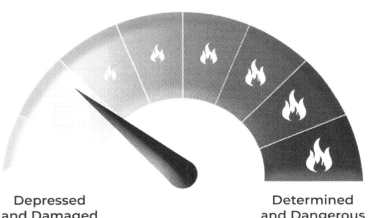

Depressed
and Damaged

Determined
and Dangerous

SECTION TWO

ACCEPTING THE TRUTH

"It takes years as a woman to unlearn what you have been taught to be sorry for. It takes years to find your voice."

— Amy Poehler

7

THE ILLUSION

With all that had happened, I felt like I had lost everything. Obviously, I had my friends and my family and for that I was so incredibly grateful but I still felt like I had something to prove.

As with most "high achievers", we're always striving for more and when we feel like our self-esteem is being knocked or we feel low, we push to achieve more and that's exactly what I did.

I focused on my dream of becoming a director at 25 and I let that fuel me forward. I visualised being the head of a department, having my own office and being able to help people more than ever before!

I threw myself into my work to prove to myself that actually I was worth something, to prove that I was valuable and that I was good at what I do.

Things felt great, I transferred to our office in Luxembourg, learnt a new language, catapulted my career and travelled across Europe at weekends. At the time, I genuinely thought everything was fine but now that I look back, my coping mechanism wasn't exactly healthy.

Every time I felt down I pushed myself back into my work and it was a reoccurring thing. The more down I got, the more work I took on. The lower I felt, the more work I took on, over and over.

I believe that this was one of the reasons I achieved a lot at such a young age because I didn't do anything else. I didn't let myself get close to anyone. I didn't let myself get distracted. It was just work, eat, sleep, repeat.

About a year after my relationship ended, I was offered my dream job, amazing money, incredible experience and so much potential. I felt like I was finally getting back on track!

Chloë Bisson, Director of a global fund manager. I gave my business cards out to everyone and anyone that would take them.

Becoming a Director at 24 years old was and is still one of my proudest achievements.

I'd worked intensely long hours, dedicated my life to work for over 6 years and reached my goal… or so I thought.

But then it hit me, the goal I'd be working so tirelessly for was done, what now?

I didn't know this at the time but the cracks of my relationship drama that I had painted over were beginning to reappear and this time I couldn't ignore them.

8

DENIAL

Denial is the first of the five stages of grief created by Elisabeth Kübler-Ross and David Kessler.

Up until this point, I had no idea that I was in denial. In fact, I didn't even realise that I was grieving.

Looking back, it was clear that I was grieving. Not only for the loss of my partner, the trust and the life we had but also grieving for the person I had been that I had now left behind.

But at the time, I had no idea.

In my mind things were fine.

In my mind it had happened for a reason.

In my mind I was over it.

I was in serious denial.

Denial is a survival mechanism that helps up to cope with loss and helps us to pace our emotions and feelings of grief. It is nature's way of letting in only as much as we can handle at one time.

There is a grace in denial, or at least that was what I was telling myself.

9

REALITY SHOCK

It was a Wednesday morning. My alarm went off, I hit the snooze button again and all I could feel was my stomach churning.

I ran to the bathroom and hovered over the toilet but nothing happened. I'd felt queasy all week but no matter how many times I ran to the bathroom, I couldn't be sick.

I turned the TV on and started getting ready for work. As I was listening to the news, I heard a young girl being interviewed on the BBC talking about how she was so glad she went to the doctor and hadn't felt sick since.

I couldn't tell you what the interview was about, all I can remember was thinking "that's exactly what's happening to me!".

On the way to work I called up the clinic and booked an appointment for lunch time with my doctor.

Dr Redshaw was my Mum's doctor and had been my doctor for over 10 years. She was incredibly understanding and had the patience of a saint, well she needed it to put up with us two.

My Mum had been at the gym and came up to meet me at the doctors. I thought she was as clueless as me, little did I know there was a reason she came with me.

Dr Redshaw asked me what I was visiting for and I explained my symptoms.

"I'm constantly feeling sick. Every morning I wake up and my stomach is in knots and I have to force myself to get out of bed. As soon as the evening comes, the sickness has gone but I'm absolutely exhausted, I'm constantly tired no matter how much I sleep."

In the past I had suffered with a lung condition and troublesome cough due to too much acid in my stomach and so I thought she would just prescribe the same tablets as she did before.

But I couldn't have been more wrong.

"It sounds to me like you may be suffering with depression, Chloë".

I'm sorry what? Depression? I'm the most positive person I know!

There was no way she could be right.

What could I possibly be depressed about?

I've got my dream job.

I've been travelling around Europe.

I've just moved back to Jersey and into a beautiful new flat.

There was no way she could be right.

"I'm going to sign you off for the rest of the week and I'll give you a call on Friday to see how you're doing"

I honestly thought she'd gone mad.

"Over the next few days, spend some time reading these leaflets and we will talk on Friday."

I don't think anything she said after that actually registered in my brain.

I was in shock.

"It's going to get worse before it gets better Chloë, but you'll get there" she said as I was walked out of the room.

10

DEPRESSION?

As defined by the World Health Organisation ("WHO"), depression is a common mental disorder, characterised by sadness, loss of interest or pleasure, feelings of guilt or low self-worth, disturbed sleep or appetite, feelings of tiredness and poor concentration.

However, I had a very different type of depression and I didn't have the "usual" signs and symptoms. I was the complete opposite.

I never wanted to be at home on my own. I was constantly going out, constantly making impulsive decisions and I was more determined than ever.

That's probably part of the reason I was so clueless.

It's often said that depression results from a chemical imbalance but that figure of speech doesn't capture how complex the disease actually is.

According to a study published by Harvard Medical School, research suggests that it isn't as simple as having too much or too little of certain brain chemicals. There are many things that can cause depression, including faulty mood regulation by the brain, genetic vulnerability, stressful life events, medications and medical problems.

So, you can see why it's more than just a "chemical imbalance" and why it can be so difficult to treat.

According to WHO, there were more than 300 million people living with depression in 2017.

I dread to think what that number is now.

11

ACKNOWLEDGING IT

Well she was right. It definitely got worse before it got better.

After the appointment, my Mum took me for some lunch and asked me how I felt about what the doctor had said.

"She's way off, Mum. There's no way I could be depressed".

That was the end of that conversation. My Mum knew I wasn't ready yet, little did I know I was about to be hit in the face with a big punch of reality.

I woke up in the morning and it hit me like a ton of bricks.

Dr Redshaw was absolutely right.

It was like all of my feelings that I had hidden from myself all came at once.

I felt sick… again.
I felt stupid… again.

I felt confused… again.

I couldn't eat…

I couldn't talk…

All I could do was cry… again.

I realised how unwell I'd been by not dealing with my emotions and how much I was in denial.

I realised how much I'd buried myself in my work to avoid the realisation of what happened.

Most importantly, I realised how hurt I'd been and how I hadn't let myself deal with it.

I'd gone straight from shock to survival mode and put on a brave face to everyone around me. I'd focused on appearing strong rather than actually dealing with it.

I'd prioritised forgiving others rather than actually healing myself.

Yes, forgiving Dean and Nina was a huge part of my healing process but I hadn't actually forgiven myself for being affected by it.

What.

The.

F*ck.

Right on cue, as promised, the call came on the Friday afternoon.

"Hi Chloë, it's Dr Redshaw, how are you feeling?"

I couldn't even string a sentence together. As soon as I heard her voice, I burst into tears.

She was incredible. She booked me in for an appointment on the following Monday and gave me some resources to help me over the weekend.

I still remember that moment like it was yesterday.

It was there and then that my life truly changed.

12

A CONVERSATION WITH MYSELF
– PART 2

Then me: "How could I be depressed and have no idea? How stupid could I be?"

Now me: "It's not stupid, it was your way of coping. You were protecting yourself from the pain."

Then me: "But how could I be so wrong about what was going on in my own mind?"

Now me: "You weren't wrong, you just hadn't allowed yourself to deal with it yet."

Then me: "But it's been over a year. What if I can't get better?"

Now me: "You will. The main thing is that you are dealing with it now and getting the help you need"

Then me: "But what if I never get back to being as strong as I was?"

Now me: "But what if you get even stronger?"

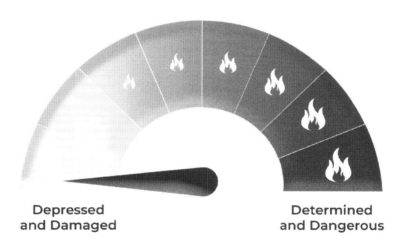

Depressed
and Damaged

Determined
and Dangerous

SECTION THREE

THE JOURNEY BACK

"I don't like to gamble, but if there's one thing I'm willing to bet on, it's myself."

— Beyoncé

13

WHAT IF

The next month was probably one of the most difficult months of my life. It was a rollercoaster of emotions. One minute I would feel completely normal and then the next minute I'd be crying because I burnt my toast.

I know it sounds funny now but there is a big difference between acknowledging it and accepting it.

I had acknowledged that something was happening to me but inside a little part of me was still fighting it and refused to accept it.

I was an emotional wreck and the worst thing was I felt like it was all my fault.

"Maybe if I hadn't stuck my head in the sand and dealt with it head on I wouldn't be as bad."

"Maybe if I hadn't moved away I would have had more people around me to see it."

Lots of "what ifs" and "maybes" were constantly floating around my mind. I didn't know at the time but this is what is known as Bargaining, another one of the five stages of Grief.

The bargaining stage is characterised by attempting to negotiate with something you feel, whether realistically or not, to have some control over the situation.

Once again, I was trying to be in control.

But, no matter how hard I tried, I couldn't find the determination to do anything.

Depression affected my life in every way possible. It was like a heavy grey cloud hovering over me at all times. A cloud that was there purely to block out the sunlight, make everything feel dark and gloomy, constantly leaving me on edge that at any point I could break down and the heavens would open.

The first few weeks I cried a lot. I felt like I'd spent the year taking leaps forward and in a matter of weeks I was being sucked backwards.

I moved back into the first apartment I bought when I was 21, which felt like a big enough step back itself, and in total, I was signed off as "unfit to work" for six months.

SIX MONTHS!

For someone who had worked so hard for years to build her career, it was heart breaking.

I felt like everything I had built was gone.

Slowly I started telling people that were close to me, my Dad, my best friends, my family members and everyone dealt with it in their own way.

I thought I had a hard time accepting it until I saw how some of my loved ones dealt with it.

"You're not depressed, you just need a holiday"

"I thought you'd have been crying more though if you were depressed"

"It's just because you've been burning the candle at both ends"

They didn't want to believe that there was another side to me.
A side that wasn't so determined.

A side that wasn't so strong.

A side that needed help.

I realised that many of them were in denial, just like I was.

14

THINGS YOU SHOULDN'T SAY

When I was at my lowest point, laughing was non-existent. Even a smile was hard to find. But one day I was reading Reasons To Stay Alive by Matt Haig, a self-help book that someone had recommended to me and something changed.

Reading page after page, wondering why I was bothering when, out of nowhere, I found myself laughing. Not just laughing silently but actually laughing out loud!

Still to this day I remember exactly what it was that made me laugh.

At the time I was reading it just to pass the time but this book turned out to be one of the main drivers for my recovery.

It described everything exactly as I had experienced it.

This page, in particular, was unbelievably true.

> **Things people say to depressives that they don't say in other life-threatening situations**
>
> 'Come on, I know you've got tuberculosis, but it could be worse. At least no one's died.'
>
> 'Why do you think you got cancer of the stomach?'
>
> 'Yes, I know, colon cancer is hard, but you want to try living with someone who has got it. Sheesh. Nightmare.
>
> 'Oh, Alzheimer's you say? Oh, tell me about it, I get that all the time.'
>
> 'Ah, meningitis. Come on, mind over matter.'
>
> 'Yes, yes, your leg *is* on fire, but talking about it all the time isn't going to help things, is it?'
>
> 'Okay. Yes. Yes. Maybe your parachute has failed. But chin up.'

15

UNDERSTANDING MY NEEDS

When reality finally hit me, I felt absolutely clueless about what was going on in my brain. I just wanted to understand what was happening and no one seemed to be able to tell me.

Everyone I spoke to just recommended self-help books for me to read.

I didn't mind at first because I knew they were only trying to help, but after hearing it over and over, all I could think was "if someone offers me one more self-help book I'm going to tell them to shove it up their ***".

I didn't want any more self-help books.

I didn't want sympathy.

I didn't want to meditate.

I didn't want to relax.

I just wanted to understand exactly what was going on. I wanted to know physically, emotionally and scientifically, what was happening to my mind.

I stumbled upon Maslow's *Hierarchy of Needs* and it felt like I'd finally found something that made sense with what I was going through. It wasn't specifically about depression but it helped me understand why I was feeling so damaged.

Maslow's *Hierarchy of Needs* is a theory based on five types of human needs; physiological, safety, love and belonging, esteem and self-actualization.

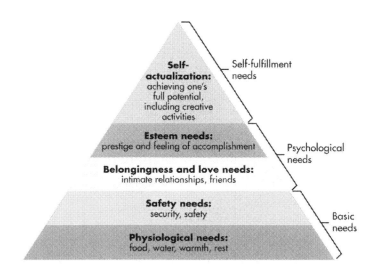

The pyramid symbolises the order in which the needs must be satisfied before attending to the needs at the next level.

Everything finally started to make sense.

In the past I had satisfied most of my needs and was working on self-actualization.

Self-actualization needs are focused on self-fulfilment, seeking personal growth and realising personal potential. This was where I had been for years before it all changed.

But with everything that happened, I lost my self-esteem, I lost my sense of belonging, I lost my relationship, I lost my home and I lost my stability. All of a sudden, my human needs for esteem, love and belonging and safety were not met.

I went crashing from the top of the pyramid to the bottom.

But instead of listening to my instincts, I continued to push myself to achieve self-fulfilment even though my basic needs weren't being met.

No wonder I felt so damaged.

It all made sense.

I knew what I had to do now.

I had to focus on getting better, starting at the bottom of the pyramid. I had to focus on resting, eating well and meeting my basic human needs.

I had to be my number one priority.

It was a really difficult thing to do.

Going from being someone that made time for everyone and being so empathic, I felt I was being selfish for focusing on myself.

Looking back on it now, I can see how irrational that thought was but it felt so real. I felt incredibly self-absorbed but it was what I needed to do and it was what I did.

16

THINGS YOU SHOULD SAY

Let's be honest, there are no magic words that will make a depressed person feel better and it can be tough to be around someone struggling and not knowing what to say.

But there are things that we need to hear when we are struggling:

 "I'm here for you"

 "It's not your fault"

 "You're not a burden"

"Take as long as you need"

"I don't think you're crazy"

 "You don't need to do anything that makes you uncomfortable"

"Everything is going to be OK"

 "I love you"

Remember, you don't always need to have the answer to our problems, just knowing that you're there and that we have your support no matter what can be enough.

17

HELLO RAGE

I've always been a determined person and, at times, a little feisty but I'd never felt true anger until I began to face my depression.

It was like I went from crying to screaming in a matter of minutes and was like something I'd never felt before.

I'd get angry at the smallest of things.

In fact the word anger doesn't do it enough justice. It wasn't anger, it was pure *rage*.

I didn't know at the time but anger was part of my healing process, the next stage in the five stages of grief.

What a rollercoaster.

The truth is that anger has no limits. You can feel anger towards your friends, your family and even yourself.

I had all of the above.

My Mum would tell me she had to go to see my Step-Dad and I'd be furious.

My friends would ask me to do something for them and I'd be fuming that they'd even asked.

It felt like I was burning inside. All I wanted to do was scream from the top of my lungs but no matter what I did I just couldn't release the rage.

What was happening to me?

People often consider anger as a bad thing but anger can also be strength.

It acts as something to hold on to, something to keep you moving forward and can act as an outlet for pain.

That's the most important part of the process though – letting it go.

The anger acts as a place to channel your grief and let it out and that's exactly what happened to me.

It didn't last long. No more than a couple of weeks.

But it was long enough for me to realise I still had a long way to go to get back to being me.

18

ASKING FOR HELP

So, this was really happening.

I actually had depression.

I knew I wouldn't be able to get through it on my own. My Mum and Dad were great and my friends were very supportive but I knew I needed someone with more professional experience.

My Doctor referred me to a psychologist but, even with my health insurance, it was a minimum of 8 weeks to wait until I'd be invited for my first appointment – not great.

My Aunty Fran is a qualified coach and trainer but I didn't really understand what that all meant. I just knew that she helped people!

What an understatement.

Fran has the ability to listen without judgement, provide strategies not just sympathy and offer support when it's needed the most.

She came over the same night I messaged her and we talked a lot.

I told her everything that had been going on with me and what the doctor had said. I felt like I'd been talking for hours.

She had two exercises that she wanted to do with me to see if it would help.

"What are your core values and beliefs?" she asked.

I was absolutely clueless.

My values?

My beliefs?

Do I even have those?

I was completely oblivious to what she was talking about.

"Core values are the principles that we live our lives by, they determine how we act, how we feel and what is important to us" she explained.

All I kept thinking was that I didn't feel like I had any.

I didn't know what it was like to have values.

I was just living as I'd been told to do.

She asked me to write down everything that was important to me, as many things as I could think of and then reduce it down to my top five.

My mind went blank.

The saddest part was I couldn't even think about one thing that was important to me. I know now that was the depression talking.

The second exercise we did was The Wheel of Life, a circle that displays your level of balance and satisfaction in a range of areas.

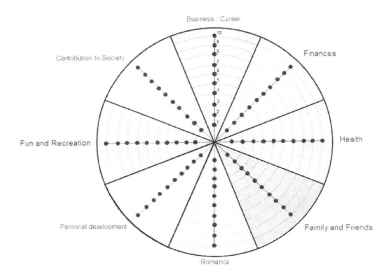

The Wheel of Life ®

The concept is that each category is scored from 1 to 10, 1 being very bad and 10 being very good. All scores are then plotted on the diagram and connected.

The lower the number, the more improvement that category needs.

I remember when I first started doing this exercise, I kept calling it the Spider Web because mine didn't look like a wheel at all!

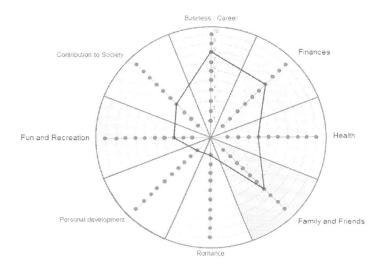

The Wheel of Life ®

It didn't take long to realise that this was very similar to the "to-do list" I wrote when I first broke up with Dean, except this time I was considering things I'd never thought about before, like fun, personal development and contribution.

This exercise opened my eyes. I realised I had tunnel vision for so long, focusing on one part of my life – my career.

I realised that, even despite my depression, there was a clear lack of personal development and contribution in my life. They were the guiding principles that changed my career path forever.

Fran and I spoke for hours that first night and met up weekly as I progressed through the exercises.

Whilst it was only a few weeks, it was a defining moment of my journey back to being me.

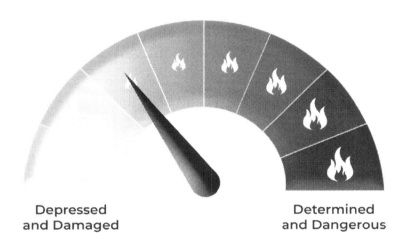

Depressed
and Damaged

Determined
and Dangerous

RIDING THE ROLLERCOASTER

"The most courageous act is still to think for yourself aloud."

— Coco Chanel

19

TALKING TO A PSYCHOLOGIST

After 8 weeks of waiting, my appointment finally arrived and I felt quite nervous.

I'd done a lot of work with Fran and I was feeling a lot better. I was worried the psychologist would dig deeper again and undo all of the progress I'd made.

But it was not what I had imagined at all.

I walked into her room and it was totally different to what I expected. I imagined it to be like something you see on the TV with the reclining beds for the patients to lie on and reflect over painful memories.

It was totally different.

It was just a normal office, with a big desk. She sat on one side of the desk and I sat on the other.

"So Chloë, tell me what's been going on with you?"

I told her everything that had happened over the past year.

"I see. Can you tell me a bit about you, your background and your family?".

It felt strange to me talking about something other than the depression but I went along and gave her all of the information that she'd asked for.

"Ok I'm going to introduce you to a strategy that I think will be really helpful for you."

That was it.

That was the end of the questions.

No 'and how does that make you feel?' like I was expecting.

In fact, we didn't really dig into deep emotions or events at all. We didn't even discuss the events that led up to my depression – not that I can remember.

She introduced me to a technique known as Cognitive Behavioural Therapy ("CBT"), a treatment that focuses on how your thoughts, beliefs and attitudes affect your feelings and behaviour.

It combines examining the things you think (cognitive) and examining the things you do (behaviour).

She explained it to me using a story of four men stepping in dog poo – Strange, I know but keep reading.

The first man steps in the dog poo and thinks to himself "Why does this always happen to me? I'm so hopeless I can't even walk properly" as he walks home sulking.

The second man steps in the dog poo and thinks to himself "Who put that there? I'm going to strangle the dog who put that there!". He kicks a nearby rubbish bin and shouts at the dog as he walks past.

The third man steps in the dog poo and thinks to himself "Oh no I'm going to be filthy. How will I ever get it off my shoe? I bet those people over there are laughing at my stupidity". He blushes and rushes around trying to clean it off.

The fourth man steps in the dog poo and thinks to himself "What a pain. Oh well I walk this way often and I rarely step in dog poo". He wipes it off and walks off.

This story illustrates how the same event can occur but the outcome we take can be completely different based on our thoughts.

The first man's thoughts triggered feelings of sadness and worthlessness which led him into going home and sulking.

The second man's thoughts triggered feelings of aggression and anger which led him to go kick a rubbish bin and shout at the dog.

The third man's thoughts triggered feelings of anxiety and paranoia which led him to go rushing around trying to clean it off as quickly as he could.

The fourth man's thoughts triggered feelings of slight irritation yet carelessness which led him to wiping it off and forgetting about it.

CBT shows us how the way we think about events will distinguish how we act.

The psychologist asked me to make a note of every intense thought I had over the next 7 days and document my actions in the same way:

- What event happened that caused that thought?

What was the thought?

How did it make me feel?

How did I react?

Before I knew it, the session was over. We'd spent about 10 minutes discussing my situation and about 50 minutes going through the strategy.

I went away and did exactly what I was told to do.

I only had 2 more sessions with the psychologist after that and it was exactly what I needed.

No more bullsh*t.

No more sympathy.

Just strategies.

20

KNOWING TOO MUCH

I thought that as soon as I can fully understand what's going on in my mind the only way is up.

Unfortunately, that wasn't the case – well not straight away.

I learnt a lot about my brain, my depression and the way my thought patterns impacted my actions but with this came a new awareness.

An awareness that I had been living my life absolutely clueless on what was going on in my brain.

That awareness turned into fear and that fear turned into anxiety.

What if there was more that I didn't know about?

What if it happens again?

Every slight change in my emotion, I noticed. I became almost obsessed with the rollercoaster of my emotions, analysing them each and every day.

This was the first sign and it spiralled from there.

I found myself feeling anxious and nervous about the smallest of things.

I found myself feeling uncomfortable around my friends and family and just wanting to be on my own.

This was the first time that I felt like this. I'd never felt like I wanted to be on my own, until now.

I know now that was the social anxiety kicking in.

Social anxiety is the fear of being judged and evaluated negatively by other people, leading to feelings of inadequacy, inferiority, self-consciousness, embarrassment, humiliation and depression.

According to the Social Anxiety Institute, studies have recently pegged social anxiety disorder as the third largest psychological disorder in the US, after depression and alcoholism.

Great.

I'm lucky enough to deal with two of the top three psychological disorders at the same time.

Wonderful.

But how could I have social anxiety?

I've spent years talking at training events and in front of large groups without even breaking a sweat.

What was going on with me now.

I still remember the first time I felt it. I'd been invited for a drink with a few close friends on a Thursday evening. Nothing huge, just a small thing to get me out of the house.

I remember feeling sick with nerves.

Even with my depression, I'd never felt anxious about leaving the house.

This feeling was totally new to me.

I found myself questioning everything about the night ahead.

Who will be there?

What if I have to meet someone that I hadn't met before?

What if someone asks about how I'm doing?

What if someone makes a joke and I don't laugh?

What if I see someone from work and they ask where I've been?

I felt like I needed to know *everything*.

I needed to know who else was going.

I needed to know what bar we were going to.

I needed to know what table we would sit at.

I even needed to know what seat I would sit on at the table.

It was *that* intense and it was only the beginning.

21

TWO EXTREMES

It is estimated that about 85% of people in the US living with depression also suffer from an anxiety.

85 percent.

There I was thinking I was the odd one out when in fact I was in the majority.

We know that depression is a feeling of low self-worth, feeling of tiredness and loss of interest in anything.

Well anxiety is the opposite.

It's an intense feeling of worry, nervousness or unease about something with an uncertain outcome. It can cause people to feel on edge, rarely relaxed and insomniac in some cases.

You can see the conflict.

One takes away all of your motivation and drive to do anything, but the other makes you constantly do that activity and overthink it.

Most people living with anxiety and depression are described as Type-A personalities or overachievers.

Doesn't that sound familiar…

It was like I was on a seesaw that never stopped.

One minute I wouldn't feel like doing anything and the next I would be terrified that if I missed something, I'd be further behind than I already was.

It was like they were constantly fighting with each other.

From one extreme to the other.

I know everyone said it would get worse but I never expected it to be quite this bad.

22

WHAT PEOPLE SAY VS WHAT YOU HEAR

"How are you feeling?"

"Shouldn't you be better by now?"

"You're looking so much better now"

"You looked a mess before"

"Wow that's different to the way I've heard it described before."

"You're wrong."

"Have you tried any relaxation techniques or meditation?"

"Come on, mind over matter."

"I'm glad you're feeling better already"

"Clearly it wasn't as bad as you made it out to be"

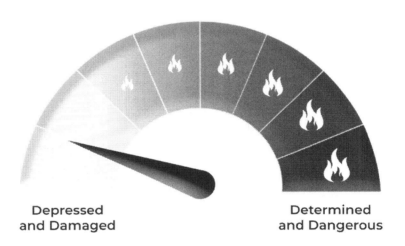

Depressed
and Damaged

Determined
and Dangerous

SECTION FIVE

LEARNING TO SMILE AGAIN

"There is no greater pillar of stability than a strong, free, and educated woman."

— Angelina Jolie

23

PERSPECTIVE

When you have any mental illness, perspective completely disappears.

The smallest things can feel like the world has ended and you completely lose the concept of perspective.

Even with the smallest problem, I was overthinking everything.

I tried to use the techniques I'd learnt with my depression but how do you do apply Cognitive Behavioural Therapy to something that hasn't happened yet?

I was stressing.

I was overthinking.

I would even stress about how much I was overthinking.

It felt like a weed with roots. As soon as one root developed, it spread to create more roots and those roots created more roots, until the weed was so entrenched it was impossible to pull out.

It was exhausting.

I knew I had to come up with a way of dealing with it. I didn't need to stop the worrying all together but I had to stop my brain analysing every possible scenario.

So, I went back to the basics.

"In this situation, what's the realistic best case scenario?"

"Can I handle that outcome?"

"In this situation, what's the realistic worst case scenario?"

"Can I handle that outcome?"

The truth was I could always handle both. We can always handle what life throws at us but I wasn't strong enough to see that then.

Once I'd ascertained that I could handle the best case scenario and the worst case scenario I knew I would be able to handle anything that happened in between.

It sounds so simple but it's such a powerful technique. It didn't matter whether I was worrying about not having enough money to buy milk or not being able to attend my best friend's wedding – this technique worked.

It didn't matter whether I could put the problem into perspective or not, this technique worked all the same.

In the cases where I didn't believe in myself enough, I'd continue on with the exercise.

"If I can't handle the worst case, what needs to change?"

"What do I need to do?"

This helped me realise that even if I couldn't handle the worst case scenario, there was always something I could do to change that.

I always had more control over the situation than I thought.

I never lost control, I simply forgot I had it.

24

THE FIRST KISS

Starting to feel a bit more myself, I faced the next hurdle – my first night out since my depression had kicked in.

It was a Friday night and a few of the girls decided to get all dressed up and go for a few drinks but I didn't know what to expect.

It was my first time actually going out for a night out in over 3 months.
It was my first time drinking alcohol in over 3 months.

It was my first time doing anything really, in over 3 months.

But it wasn't as scary as I thought it would be.

As we ordered our drinks at the first bar, we noticed straight away that we were starting to get some attention. Well we were 5 single girls all dressed up, having a laugh, with no guys in sight so I guess that was to be expected.

We vowed it would be a girl's only night.

No matter who approached us, who offered us drinks, we vowed it would be a night of drinking, dancing and laughing, just us girls.

That lasted all night.

To be honest, we were getting quite rude by the end of the night as we were fed up of being interrupted when we just wanted to have fun as a group of girls.

It was 1:55am and the club was closing in about 5 minutes.

Some guy had been looking over at me for a little while and I just smiled and carried on dancing with the girls.

I didn't recognise him.

I was intrigued.

Considering Jersey is a very small island and everyone knows everyone, how had I not seen this guy before.

He came over and asked me if he could dance with me.

I thought – you've got some balls to come over on your own to a group of girls and ask me to leave them to dance with you.

As I looked down at my watch, I said to him:

"You've got 5 minutes to impress me".

I still have no idea where that came from.

I don't know if it was the drink talking or being fed up of being interrupted by guys that night.

But whatever he did, it worked.

For those 5 minutes, we danced, we laughed and we even had a cheeky kiss.

The lights came on and we all left the club. I went one way with my friends and he went the other.

What had just happened?

I had gone out, got dressed up, drank alcohol, stayed out until 2am and kissed a complete stranger.

It was nice to just have fun and not have time to think about anything. I felt, dare I say it, normal.

His name was Cedric and it turns out the reason I hadn't met him before was because he was from France and fairly new to the island.

I did give him my number but I wasn't expecting him to actually message me.

Monday came and he asked if I wanted to meet him for a drink that night and I said yes.

But as the hours past, I got more and more nervous, knowing that I would be meeting him when I was sober.

I felt physically sick.
What if I don't like him?

What if he doesn't like me?

What if there's nothing to talk about?

What if he tries to kiss me?

Why did I say yes?

The thoughts didn't stop.

It got to 2 minutes before he was supposed to meet me outside my house and I froze.

He called me.

I didn't pick up.

He texted me.

"I'm outside your house when you're ready".

10 minutes past and I was still sat on my couch.

3 more missed calls later and I messaged him to say I couldn't make it.

"What? Why?" he asked.

I just completely ignored him.

A day past and I messaged to say how sorry I was and that 'something came up'.

We rescheduled for the next night but the same thing happened.

All day I was panicking about what to wear, where we would go, what if I saw someone I knew, what if he tries for more.

It came to the time he was picking me up, he called and I completely ignored him, again.

He messaged me a long message of confusion and frustration. I wanted to tell him it wasn't his fault but I just couldn't find the words.

I couldn't get past the worry, the pressure, the fear.

Looking back, I know it was the anxiety but I just couldn't get past it. I was absolutely terrified of letting anyone in.

25

THE FEAR

Letting someone in again after a breakup can be really difficult.

Whether or not you're feeling anxious, insecure, distrusting or worthless, the fear is intense.

Heartbreak isn't just a metaphor.

Studies by the University of Amsterdam showed that breakups actually affect the nervous system, which involves sexual arousal, digestion and regulation of internal organs, like the heart. It's a physical disorder.

So, it's natural to want to avoid feeling heartbroken again and what better way than to avoid feeling anything at all – right?

It's like forgetting to put sun cream on and getting burnt to a crisp on the first day of your holiday. You wouldn't go out the next day, sit in the sun without sun cream on and wait to get burnt again would you?

That was exactly what I was feeling, except I didn't just have stronger sun cream on, I'd locked myself in a room with no windows and no sunlight so there was absolutely no chance of getting sunburnt.

But we're obviously not talking about getting a tan.

It's a genuine fear, the dread of getting hurt again.

26

KEEP MOVING

Weeks went past and life went on.

Considering I'd never seen Cedric in Jersey before, it was like he was everywhere I went now.

I'd be walking down the road and see him on the other side.

I'd be leaving a shop and see him walking in.

It was like a constant reminder of what I'd done so I tried to forget about him.

I threw myself into the gym and kept myself busy.

People always make comments about women who come out of relationships and decide to start going to the gym 'to look good to spite the man' and 'to show him what he's lost'.

But this concept really frustrates me.

Why does everything have to be about a man? Why can't a woman just want to look good for herself?

In fact it's our natural instinct.

We have instincts designed to help us survive but when we feel broken and alone we are vulnerable. Our natural instinct is to protect ourselves by getting strong again to increase our chances of survival.

It isn't about us getting back at the man that broke our heart or about craving love or affection, it's to protect us and ensure our survival for the future, not to mention the health benefits of stimulating endorphins which are natural stress relievers.

There's something really relaxing working out in an empty gym in the middle of the day when most people are at work.

I could start my sessions whenever I wanted.

Go on whatever machines I wanted.

Do whatever I wanted.

Finally, I felt in control.

I went every day for the next month and it became my sanctuary.

As I felt my body strengthen, my mind did too.

I felt more relaxed.

I felt more comfortable with what had happened.

I felt more me.

Although I didn't feel strong at the time, looking back now I know that overcoming my depression was one of the strongest moments of my life.

27

BEING REUNITED

I was out on a night out for my best friend's birthday and it was the usual Jersey night out – drinks at a few different bars and then onto the main nightclub.

I was having such a good night with my friends and best of all, no drama.

I came back from the toilet and walked to the dance floor where I realised, I couldn't see any of my friends.

I looked all around the dance floor but I couldn't see them.

I looked to see if I could see anyone at the bar but I still couldn't see anyone.

As I got my phone out to call them, I looked to the right and saw him. Cedric was stood right next to me with his friend.

SH*T.

I felt sick.

My heart started racing.

SH*T SH*T SH*T! Where *is* everyone?!

As I tried to look for my friends but avoid looking in his direction, he looked up and saw me.

SH*T.

Well I've got to say something now so I turned around.

"Hey! How are you?" I asked awkwardly.

He looked so good.

White shirt, blue jeans and brown shoes. He looked so sharp and so attractive.

What had I done.

We ended up chatting most of the night, having a few drinks and laughing together. I saw my friends again and introduced them to him.

Obviously, they already knew who he was because I had told them about the whole thing but they played dumb.

At the end of the night, we started walking back to my flat.

I was ruthless.

"Don't even think anything is happening tonight".

He just laughed.

We ended up being awake most of the night just talking and it was so nice.

When we eventually woke up, I had a message from my Dad as he was on his way to my flat – I had totally forgotten it was Father's Day!

We both got ready and went our separate ways, but I couldn't stop smiling.

A few days later he called me to see if I was free. He'd just finished at the gym and wanted to see if he could come around.

His gym was less than 5 minutes from my apartment.

I felt so sick with nerves.

I'd never seen him when I was sober.

All the "what ifs" started to come into my head again.

But before I gave myself the chance to freak out, I said yes.

I didn't even have time to put makeup on, but I thought, I've got nothing to lose.

So, he came around and we had such a good night. No pressure, just chatting and laughing. He had only been in Jersey for a few months so we didn't know anything about each other.

He had no idea who I was, he had no idea about my cheating ex and he had no idea about my depression.

It was so refreshing to meet someone that didn't know anything about me.

It was like a completely fresh start and I wasn't about to ruin it.

He told me that he was planning on leaving Jersey in September to move to London. I wasn't sure if I was disappointed because I liked him or relieved because there was no pressure of commitment – one less thing to worry about.

So, our summer romance started, both knowing that neither of us were looking for anything serious.

We went for our first date on the beach. The weather was amazing. We bought some cheap snacks and sandwiches from the little corner shop and lay on the beach all day.

It was perfect.

The way we met and the way I "played hard to get" became a bit of a joke between us. He didn't know why I had treated him so badly and I wasn't about to tell him – not yet.

Two weeks later, he was given a week off work unexpectedly because he had holidays he had to use. It was too expensive to go back to France at such short notice so he decided to go to London for 5 days and he asked if I wanted to come for a city break.

Why not.

I was still off work and thought there was nothing to lose. He didn't know I was signed off, he just thought I was having some time off in between jobs.

It was a big step in our relationship, dating for only a few weeks and then booking a trip away together.

But we had such a good time! We visited places, we laughed, we ate and it was exactly what we both needed.

One night, we were lying in bed talking about how much fun we'd had and Cedric called me "Dangerous". I had no idea what he meant, whether it was the language barrier or not.

I asked him over and over what he meant but he wouldn't say anything else.

Everything felt like it was coming together but I realised over that week I was really starting to get feelings for him.

Like real feelings.

Uh oh.

Depressed
and Damaged

Determined
and Dangerous

SECTION SIX

FINDING MY VOICE

"The purpose of life is to live it, to taste experience to the utmost, to reach out eagerly and without fear for newer and richer experience."

— *Eleanor Roosevelt*

28

A CONVERSATION WITH MYSELF
– PART 3

Then me: "I think I'm starting to fall for him! I don't know what to do!"

Now me: "Enjoy every minute of it and go with the flow."

Then me: "But it's been ages since I've felt this way. What if I get hurt again?"

Now me: "If that happens, you'll deal with it the same way that you've dealt with everything else so far, with determination, grace and strength."

Then me: "But what if I have to tell him about my depression?"

Now me: "You will tell him the truth and he will listen."

Then me: "But what if he thinks that I'm weak and broken?"

Now me: "But what if he sees that you're stronger for it?"

29

TELLING HIM

I thought it was scary telling someone you loved them for the first time but that seemed like nothing compared to what I was about to tell Cedric.

I was so worried.

We were still in the fun, exciting part of 'whatever we were' and I really didn't want to change that. Although having depression is nothing to be ashamed of, the instinct to hide it is so strong.

Is there even a right time to tell someone you care about that you have depression?

"We'd only been dating for a month or two so why couldn't I leave it a bit longer" I kept telling myself.

But as we talked more about our pasts, shared stories of our families and hopes for our futures, I felt like I wasn't being honest with him. There was a huge part of my life, a huge part of me that I was hiding from him.

It's part of my story and ultimately, he could take it or leave it but deep down I knew I didn't want him to leave it at all.

Either way, I knew I had to tell him.

We were sat in my living room and we were talking about the night we met and how far we'd come. He made a joke about how I had left him after that night and what might have happened if I hadn't "fobbed him off".

After all, he had no idea why I had treated him so badly, he just thought I was playing hard to get but there was so much more to it than that.

I sat him down and told him I needed to tell him something.

"So, this is really hard and I don't really know how to say this, but the reason I originally treated you so badly was because I was suffering with depression".

There I said it.

As soon as I said it, it was like the flood gates had opened and I couldn't stop talking. I told him everything that had happened.

Before I gave him the chance to say anything, I told him that I didn't need him to be my rock or stay with me to support me. I just simply needed him to know.

I can't remember what happened next other than he didn't say much. I think it was because he didn't know what to say.

He mentioned that he hadn't been close to anyone with a mental illness before and so he didn't really know what it was like.

The main thing I can remember was him saying if I ever needed some time to myself, just to tell him and he'd understand.

He didn't ask any questions.

He just listened.

And that was it.

He didn't look at me any different.

He didn't speak to me any different.

He didn't treat me any different.

Everything was exactly the same as it had been before.

What a relief.

Having any illness, whether physical or mental, isn't anyone's fault and being open about it is incredibly brave.

Depression may be a part of me, but it isn't all of me and Cedric helped me see that.

30

ACCEPTANCE

Many people think once they've acknowledged their mental illness, the hard bit is done but actually acknowledging it and accepting it are two very different things.

Acknowledging is usually early in the healing process which helps you move out of denial, whereas acceptance is the final hurdle, the final stage in the five stages of grief.

It's not necessarily about being alright or "over it", it's about accepting the reality that it's happened, recognising that this new reality is permanent.

We learn to live with it.

Acceptance doesn't come overnight. It's not like waking up one morning and jumping out of bed singing with the birds.

It's comes in bits and pieces, dribs and drabs.

Instead of denying our struggle, we listen to our needs; we move, we change, we grow, we evolve. We do what we need to do to get by and that's OK.

I can't tell you at what point I had accepted my mental illness, other than the moment I realised it.

I was talking to my friends and they were talking about one of our friend's relationships. They were making comments about her boyfriend, how they're not good together and how she'd changed.

Where previously I probably would have joined in and shared my opinion, I realised I didn't have one.

I just remember feeling like it was such a pointless conversation.

"If she's happy and it's not hurting anyone, what does it matter?" I said.

Since that moment, that question has been and continues to be the motto I live my life by.

It was like a wand was waved and my judgement was gone.

I didn't judge others anymore at all and I didn't care if others judged me.

Whilst the feeling of acceptance was a great feeling, there were some downsides.

I had no filter anymore.

A thought came into my head and came straight out of my mouth. If people thought I was dangerous before, they were in for a shock now.

It has caused me quite a few painful moments but it wasn't like I didn't care about anyone, I just didn't make their issue my issue.

I had built a boundary, a bubble around me. It was like no matter what was said to me or what came at me, it would hit the bubble and bounce right off.

I felt like a totally different person.

I felt free in my own mind.

31

IDENTIFYING MY PURPOSE

Seven months after being diagnosed with depression, I was back.

I was feeling like myself again.

I could confidently say that I'd stared depression in the face and I came out on top.

But what now?

I'd just been through a huge life changing experience and I'm supposed to go back into the corporate world and pretend like it never happened?

I knew so much more about myself, my goals, my values, my beliefs and I couldn't just ignore that.

Everything happens for a reason and I wanted to know my reason.

What was the benefit of going through all of this?

What was the purpose?

What was *my* purpose?

I'd never really thought before about why I was actually put on this earth.

I get that, for some people, their purpose and passion in life is obvious and clear but for me it just wasn't. I'd spent my whole life working towards a goal I never really questioned and I wasn't about to do the same thing again.

I thought to myself "what if I can use what I've learnt to help others?"

It sounded like an amazing idea but how would I make that a reality?

I had a lot of research to do but I needed to get back on my feet and get back into the workplace.

I went back to work as a training and recruitment manager in a company where I'd previously worked for a few years.

I knew their business inside and out so it was actually quite an easy transition. I spent my days talking to people, learning about them and teaching them how to grow but it felt like something was missing.

I loved working so closely with people but I felt like I was doing it to help the business, not necessarily to help the people individually.

Something didn't feel right.

So, I started digging deeper.

I reached out to a friend of a friend who worked as a workplace mentor for school leavers, sent him my CV and I asked to meet him for coffee.

We talked for hours, shared our experiences, shared our passions for helping people and it felt like someone finally knew what I was looking for.

I asked if I could do voluntary work for them to get experience but he laughed.

"You've already got plenty of experience! You've been through a lot and have picked up many skills throughout your career, you shouldn't be doing it for free."

I didn't believe him at first.

I kept thinking to myself, he's wrong.

I'm a Chartered Certified Accountant who's now working as a training manager. The only reason they gave me the job was because they knew I could do it. I don't have any qualifications relevant to mentoring or coaching.

I can't be charging people for my… what would I even call it? Coaching?

And those famous words came out of my mouth:

"I'm not good enough".

He offered for me to shadow him for a day to give me a taste of what was needed and allow me to "make my own mind up" about whether I was good enough.

So, the next chance I could, I took him up on his offer and shadowed him for a day.

I watched as he spoke to a range of students, asked them questions about how they were getting on and helped them come up with solutions to problems they were facing.

That one day helped me realise that he was right. All of my experience in the corporate world had taught me all of the skills I needed:

Listening skills.
Communication skills.
Teaching skills.
Observation skills.
And so on.

I didn't need a degree. I just needed to be me.

That was the push I needed, to know that I would absolutely love to do what they do and I actually believed that I could do it.

I realised that my purpose in life was to help people make their lives better.

But the same question remained, how?

136

32

HELPING OTHERS

So, my research began.

Turns out there are so many ways of helping others, even specific professions that offer services to help others.

I came across 5 main professions that interested me in my mission to help others; coaching, counselling, consulting, mentoring and training.

Coaching

According to the International Coach Federation coaching is defined as partnering with clients in a thought-provoking and creative process that inspires them to maximize their personal and professional potential.

With coaching, you're not expected to be an expert at a particular topic that you're coaching on, you're there to help the client to find their answers from within themselves.

I thought coaching was a great idea. It was a technique I'd used a few times as a manager but I'd love to learn more about it!

Counselling

According to the Oxford Dictionary, counselling is defined as the process of assisting and guiding clients to resolve especially personal, social, or psychological problems and difficulties.

Counselling involves looking back to issues from the past to overcome particular challenges or problems.

This was an interesting one.

I loved the idea of helping people overcome difficulties but I wasn't sure if I was patient enough to get all deep and emotional.

I know I'd suffered with depression but my determination and "take action" personality doesn't lend itself to the softly, fluffy approach so perhaps not the best option for me…

Consulting

As defined by the Business Dictionary, consulting is the act of providing expert knowledge to a third party.

As a consultant you are required to have specific knowledge on the problem faced by your client as you're relied on to understand the problem and present solutions to the client.

This was definitely another option for me as I'd spent years building up technical knowledge to be able to reach director level in my career and I knew a lot of people needed help with this.

Mentoring

As defined by Management Mentors, mentoring is a professional relationship in which an experienced person assists another in developing specific skills and knowledge.

Mentoring is also targeted purely on the future and the goals of the client and doesn't involved looking back over past experiences.

This is exactly what I was doing before; using my previous experience to help others achieve a similar goal.

I loved the idea of helping people take their life to the next level by learning from my mistakes.

Training

According to the Oxford Dictionary, training is the process of bringing a person to an agreed standard of proficiency by practice and instruction.

Training is usually focused on a particular subject matter, rather than a particular past experience. It may help towards achieving a goal once the goal is identified.

This made my decision really difficult.

My few months as a training manager made me realise how much I loved running workshops, speaking in front of big groups and teaching subjects that I'm passionate about, but this is a little less personal than being a mentor, isn't it?

There were just too many options.

But here's the secret, no one said I could only pick one.

I decided to start my business that would help others achieve a specific future goal but I would be able to step in as a Trainer, Mentor, Coach or Consultant, depending on what they needed at the time.

Like having four tools in my toolbox ready for use.

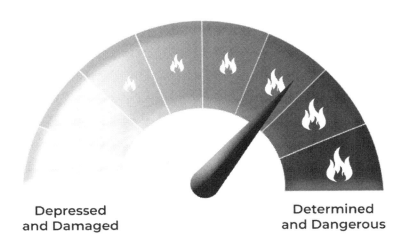

Depressed
and Damaged

Determined
and Dangerous

SECTION SEVEN

TAKING THE LEAP

"It takes a great deal of courage to stand up to your enemies, but even more to stand up to your friends."

— J.K. Rowling

33

GETTING READY

Over the next few months I studied as much as I could about the services I would offer.

I became a qualified Neuro-Linguistic Programming Practitioner, I was awarded a Diploma in Psychology and Counselling and I became a Certified Professional Coach.

I told myself I needed the qualifications before I could get started but I was wrong.

I didn't need it for the business, I needed it for me.

It was all just for that feeling that I wasn't good enough.

Yes, I learnt some interesting techniques but I realised that I'd been using it to procrastinate and avoid making the big jump.

So as soon as I finished my last course, I forced myself to commit to getting started but how?

The first thing that came to my mind that I needed was a website. I had to have a website so people can find me – right?

Wrong.

I now know that this is not the best place to start but I didn't know that at the time.

In order to have a website, I had to pick a business name and logo and so the ideas started flowing.

After working in the corporate world for so long, I knew the importance of having a company to stand behind. I kept telling myself it was best for the business if it's called something generic, but I knew that wasn't really the case.

Once again there was much more to it than that.

I knew it was more about my self-worth.

If I called it "Professional Coaching Limited", it feels a lot less scary than "Chloë Bisson Limited".

I know now that it was about having a business to hide behind.

I came up with a business name called "Three Seas Philosophy". The idea being that my principals were three C's – Challenge, Change and Conquer.

With these principles, I could help people with any problems they'd been facing, with the goal to challenge it, change it and conquer it. It seemed so obvious to me.

Before I knew it, my mind was coming up with all of these logos of waves to symbolise the three C's.

Now let me tell you a secret.

At the time I thought it was genius. Having a business name that had so much meaning and a logo that symbolised it so well.

But after years of experience, I look back now knowing it was totally the wrong decision.

No one knew what "Three Seas Philosophy" meant.

No one knew why the logo was made up of waves with three C's in it.

Here's what I've learnt since then about picking a business name:

- Make sure it's easy to write so you won't have to spell it out to people
- Avoid using words that could be written in different ways (1st and first etc)
- Keep it short
- Check what it means in other languages (and doesn't end up meaning something totally unrelated)
- Make it memorable
- Make it personal – if you're offering a service like coaching or mentoring, don't be afraid to use your own name.

As a general rule, if your business name and / or logo is hard to understand, it will be even harder for you to get clients.

I didn't know any of that at the time.

I didn't have anyone to guide me.

I just had to go with what I thought was best and that's exactly what I did.

So, now that I had a business name and a logo, I could get started on my website!

Thankfully, my Mum had a side business doing web design for local businesses. Finally, I had someone who could answer my questions.

But, how often does a daughter really listen to her Mum?

Not very often.

That's exactly what happened.

We started off building the website together, but quickly I learnt how to use her software and off I went, building a website with as much detail as I could find.

I had pages on each of my packages.

I had a long 'about me' page.

I wrote blogs on various topics.

I even embedded a 'contact us' form.

It took me weeks to pull together and I was so proud.

Little did I know no one was actually going to read any of it.

34

OPINIONS OF OTHERS

I don't know why but people are always strange when it comes to starting your own business.

I thought it was just me that had to deal with unsupportive people but over my years of experience since, I found that most entrepreneurs go through it.

Everyone seems to have an opinion on your new business.

Everyone thinks they know better than you.

I had people telling me that I shouldn't start my own business because I'd had depression in the past.

I told them that's exactly why I am.

I'm starting my business *because* I had struggled with depression in the past. I had been at the lowest points and I still managed to come back.

They didn't seem to get it.

"You can't run your own business"

"You're too nice to be a business owner"

"You've never ran a business before"

"You haven't got what it takes"

"You won't be able to do it on your own"

"Where will you get your clients from?"

"You won't make any money"

"It's too big a risk"

"What if no one buys?

"How will you make sure you can pay your bills?"

And my all-time favourite:

"Why don't you get a proper job"

It's a good thing I didn't listen to any of them.

35

THE BIG DAY

The day had come. The day I was going to launch my new business to the world.

With a services business, particularly one without a physical office, the launch is pretty simple. You don't need to have a 'Launch Party' or an office opening party as there isn't really anything to open, as such.

My launch consisted of letting people know what I was doing and opening my calendar for clients to book in.

I felt so nervous.

I was sat in my Mum's living room with Cedric, going over and over everything making sure it all worked.

My new email address was working.

My Facebook page had the correct details on.

My website had the correct prices on.

I felt sick.

Telling the world that you're launching your own business is a huge step. Opening yourself up to judgement and potential failure that everyone can watch is such a vulnerable moment.

I'd spent so long building up my strength and determination and I was about to risk it all – or at least it felt like that.

I wrote a long motivational post on my Facebook profile about why I wanted to help others and my purpose in life, including a link to my new Facebook business page.

I reread the post over and over.

Eventually, I clicked 'Post'.

I quickly clicked on my business page and started inviting my friends to like it.

"It's live!" I shouted.

People now know about my new business, about what I've spent so much of my time on!

I waited.

Nothing happened.

I waited a few hours, watched as my Facebook page got a few likes but nothing happened.

No emails.

No bookings.

Nothing.

I'm not really sure what I was expecting to happen to be honest.

I think I expected people to just start booking in to work with me.

But nothing came through.

Nothing.

36

WHAT YOU THINK YOU NEED
VS WHAT YOU ACTUALLY NEED

Clearly, I was *way* off when it came to the launch of my business.

There was a lot that I didn't need to do.

There was a lot of time wasted on things I didn't need.

There were a lot of ways that I could have made it easier.

What you think you'll need to get started:

A beautifully designed logo
A fancy website
A set of business cards
A list of your packages, beautifully designed and printed
An email address
An invoicing system

A client relationship management ("CRM") system

A bank account

A business certificate (or registration)

Any required insurance

(Usually in *that* order of importance)

What you'll actually need to get started:

A business registration

Any required insurance

A way of taking payment

That's it.

You don't necessarily need to build a website or design a fancy logo, you just need to be you and put your message out there.

I spent weeks and weeks building my website, when I could have spent weeks and weeks connecting with people.

I could have spent weeks and weeks going to networking events and putting my message out there.

I could have spent weeks and weeks actually doing my business!

37

BEING HEARD

I think it was safe to say I was a little bit disappointed by the reaction when I launched my business.

I didn't get any interest in my new services.

I didn't really know where to go from there.

A week after my launch, I woke up with a message on Facebook from a friend of Cedric's. She was working at the local newspaper and came across my posts on Facebook that Cedric had been sharing.

She wanted to interview me for the newspaper.

I was speechless.

She wants to interview *me*?

I was so excited!

Finally, I'll get an opportunity to share my message further.

We met for coffee the next day.

"So Chloë, tell me a little bit about you"

I told her about my past.

I told her about my business.

I told her about my mission for the future.

I don't think I stopped talking the whole time we were there.

She went away and wrote an article about depression in the island and included my story to show how depression doesn't have to be the end.

It's even still available in their archives:

https://www.bailiwickexpress.com/jsy/news/antidepressant-prescriptions-are-still-rise/

I was buzzing.

I told my friend about it and how it gave me even more motivation to help people.

She told me she had a friend that worked at our local BBC radio station and told me to get in touch.

She gave me her email address and I sent her an email straight away.

A few days later, I got a reply. They invited me into their studio to interview me on mental health and the importance of helping people through it.

A second interview – Already?

I couldn't stop smiling.

What will I have to say?

What if she asks me a question I don't know the answer to?

What do I wear?

"Chloë, it's a radio interview, no one will see what you're wearing" Cedric said with a smile on his face.

He was right.

I was worrying so much because this time it would be live, another step out of my comfort zone.

Cedric told me to be myself and my passion would come across and that's exactly what happened.

They asked questions and I answered them. It went so quickly and it was over before I knew it.

I still have the recording of the radio interview on my YouTube channel as a reminder of where it all started.

https://youtu.be/4yrpt9jW4ow

With all of this happening in the space of one week, I had a big realisation. Both of these opportunities came from people I knew.

The network I had already.

I had spent a lot of time creating a new website and trying to meet new people, I forgot about the value of the network I had already.

I realised that in order to make this a success, I needed to take responsibility for my message being heard, starting with people around me.

I'd been hiding from them because of the fear of being judged but actually, they were the people who would be able to help me the most.

I needed to put myself out there to them. I don't mean just by posting on my Facebook page now and then.

I had to make sure all of my friends knew my message.

I had to be *known*.

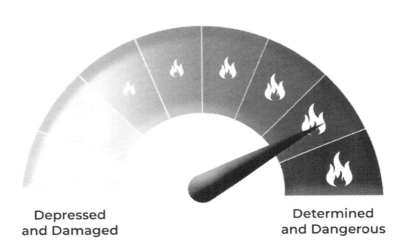

Depressed
and Damaged

Determined
and Dangerous

SECTION EIGHT

GO BIG OR GO HOME

"It's just learning not to take the first no. And if you can't go straight ahead, you go around the corner."

— Cher

38

MY FIRST CLIENT

It finally happened.

I got my first client.

I woke up one morning to an email from someone I used to work with in my last job. She had heard the interview on BBC Radio and wanted to see if I could help her.

I couldn't believe it. I had someone that was actually interested in what I could offer.

We had a call a few hours later to discuss her needs and I had a really strange feeling. On one side I felt a lot of empathy for everything she was going through and on the other I had an intense feeling of happiness because everything she said she was struggling with I knew I could help her with.

It was like a list with tick boxes and I just kept ticking.

"I feel like I've achieved a lot with my life but something is missing"

Tick.

"I want to do something with my life that will make my kids proud"

Tick.

"I want to be more than a mum, I want to be me"

Tick.

Tick.

Tick.

I knew I could help her with it all.

There's something quite surreal when someone is explaining their pain and you can predict the words to come out of their mouth next.

Not for being arrogant or over-confident.

But because you know your customer avatar so well. You know exactly the type of person you want to help.

Our call went on for an hour and at the end she asked how she could get started.

There was no fancy sales presentation or sales script. If I'm honest I think I was more excited about being able to help her than actually getting paid for it!

I offered her a 4 week coaching package, with 4 one to one coaching sessions for £99.99 as she was based in the UK.

Without evening flinching, she signed up to work with me.

I know.

It was far too cheap.

But at the time I didn't really believe that anyone would pay me anything yet.

Finding someone that was genuinely struggling and knowing with complete certainty that I could help them was incredible.

It was the best feeling in the world.

It wasn't about the money.

It was the validation.

Someone actually valued my experience and skills enough to want to pay me.

I hadn't even started working with her yet and I already felt so much fulfilment.

As planned, our sessions started. We worked through a number of exercises that I knew would benefit her; I coached her through a few problems, trained her on a few strategies and mentored her using my personal experiences.

Her transformation was incredible.

She didn't just feel better in herself. Her relationship with her partner improved, her efficiency at work improved, everything improved.

At that moment, I knew this was what I wanted to do for the rest of my life. It gave me the momentum to continue spreading my message, no matter what.

I knew that if I could help just one person a month have a transformation like hers, I would be on top of the world.

39

THE KNOWLEDGE BUSINESS INDUSTRY

According to Top University, students of English universities are required to pay anywhere from £9,250 to £38,000 per year depending on the type of degree.

Similarly, the cost for students of US universities can range from US$10,230 to US$48,510 per year depending on the type of degree.

With these sort of numbers, it's no surprise that there's been a huge increase in people choosing to educate using other methods.

According to the School of Education American University, the global education-tech industry is projected to grow to a $93.76 billion industry by 2020.

That includes things like e-courses, online coaches, education apps and online masterminds.

It's a staggering figure.

With an industry like that, it's a no brainer why so many people have transitioned into the industry over the past few years.

After not being able to afford to go to university myself, I'm personally all for the self-education industry and I believe that we can all learn a lot from people that have incredible experience and knowledge, without necessarily having the letters after their name.

Not to mention being on the other side of the table and being able to help people all over the world with the lessons we've learnt and the mistakes we've all made.

It's an amazing feeling being able to generate income for impacting people's lives.

40

SPECIALISING

So, fast forward six months and things were going really well.

I had made $12,000 in the last 12 weeks and I had helped nearly a hundred ladies through a range of areas in their lives.

I know, a hundred ladies in 36 weeks!

I was using Facebook to offer two free coaching sessions to help with whatever area they were struggling with and I met so many different people.

One person I was helping to overcome anxiety and panic attacks.

Another person I was helping to get a better job.

Another person I was helping to set up her own coaching business.

Some of them came for the two free sessions and got everything they needed straight away. Others wanted to continue to work with me on a deeper level and so my business grew.

It was such a variety and I loved it, but deep down I knew that I'd need to start specialising.

Yes I could help everyone.

Yes I could help to fix a number of problems.

But I knew that in order to be able to grow and streamline, I had to specialise and simplify my services.

What were my biggest passions?

What were my unique skills and abilities?

I knew that my strongest ability was being able to simplify even the most complicated tasks and processes. I'd learnt that through years of training people in the corporate world.

But in terms of the topic, I had learned so many more skills as I had been growing my business.

I learnt how to easily create social media content.

I learnt how to find potential clients.

I learnt how to schedule email campaigns.

And I learnt how to set it all up in a system that was easy to use.

I knew this was all information that new coaches and aspiring entrepreneurs would really benefit from, especially the ones that wanted a better quality of life.

Those clients that had watched me grow often asked me how I did it.

I didn't really know how or why but my clients were always telling me how much easier it sounded when I explained it to them.

So, I decided that had to be the direction to go in.

I was going to specialise in helping individuals to set up their own online services business with success.

Goodbye Three Seas Philosophy.

Hello Chloë Bisson.

41

A CONVERSATION WITH MYSELF – PART 4

Then me: "If I specialise, I will miss out on opportunities with new clients."

Now me: "You'll only miss out on the new clients that need something that you no longer offer."

Then me: "But I've been putting myself out there as Three Seas Philosophy. If I change now, people will think I've failed."

Now me: "People will think what they want. The important thing is that they're thinking about you and you've got their attention."

Then me: "But what if I specialise and my business goes backwards?"

Now me: "But what if you specialise and your business soars forwards?"

42

YOUR TRIBE

One of the biggest challenges that a lot of entrepreneur's face is knowing how and when to ask for help.

Often, we feel like we have to do it all on our own to be truly successful but the truth is that success is what you make it and you don't have to do it all by yourself.

Your network is your net worth after all.

I knew if I was going to take what felt like a huge leap of faith, I needed to have the right people around me.

The life of an entrepreneur can be a bit of a rollercoaster and having someone sitting next to you to hold your hand and scream with you makes it all a lot easier.

Someone that can help you when you're having a tough day and help you feel better.

Someone that can help you when you're stuck with a problem and need advice.

Someone that can keep you accountable and give you the push you need when you're avoiding something.

And even someone who can say what a load of bullsh*t when you're making excuses.

This isn't just one person that ticks all the boxes but individual people who can support you in their own way.

Those people that are rallying for you to succeed.

That's your tribe.

Part of the process of building your tribe is also removing those that are not supporting you.

Some people call them toxic people but I'm not a fan of that phrase.

I believe that everyone is acting in the best way that they can with the information that they have. I believe that there is no such thing as a toxic person, only toxic relationships, relationships that no longer serve you.

As soon as I started observing my relationships with this "filter" I could see a clear divide. Those that were supporting me with my business (even if they didn't realise it) and those that weren't.

I felt guilty and selfish for even thinking that some of my friends were not supporting me, but the truth was, just because they weren't supporting me with my business, didn't mean they weren't supporting me at all in my life.

You can still have friends in your life that aren't necessarily there for supporting you with your business, as long as you feel you are enjoying their relationship in other ways.

Maybe they're not great when it comes to your business but they're a great friend to have when you need to have time off and forget about everything for a few hours.

That's ok too.

I learnt the key was to build an awareness of who I needed in my tribe and acknowledging that I have the support I need.

As soon as I realised that I wasn't on my own, the journey got a lot easier.

I had Cedric to support me with the ups and downs and the little voice inside my head that was telling me I wasn't good enough.

I had my Mum to remind me that I'm strong enough and to push me to keep going.

I had my Aunty Fran to help me when I was stuck with a problem and needed to find the solution.

But I realised there was a gap in my inner circle.

I'd learnt a lot about running my own business from doing it myself but something was missing.

I didn't have anyone who had actually ran their own business before, especially a business that offered online services.

I knew I was ready to take my business to the next level and I needed to find someone who could show me the way.

43

GETTING A MENTOR

Getting a mentor was the moment everything changed for me.

I went from being a self-employed coach, mentor and trainer to being a business owner.

That transition in my mind was a big enough step in itself, little did I know there was much more to come.

As the incredible Tony Robbins quoted 'Business is 80% psychology and 20% strategy and therefore it's important to get the right balance between psychological support and technical support to reach your goals.

I believe that all business owners should have two types of expert support:

- A mentor to help you level up your business; and

- A coach to help you level up you.

After all, as soon as you start to grow as a person, the possibilities for your business grow too.

That's exactly what I did.

I wasn't actually looking for a coach at the time but I met an amazing woman, Judy, who had dedicated her life to help women grow as individuals. I resonated with Judy on a whole new level and it was incredible to meet someone that was as passionate about helping people as I was.

As individuals, we have many strengths but often we struggle to express them to others. If we do, we feel as if we're showing off. In some cases we can't even see our strengths because we're not appreciative of ourselves.

This is where we need someone else to pull it out of us.

That's exactly what happened to me.

Judy helped me reach a whole new level of clarity about myself. I got an incredible self-awareness and a huge realisation about my purpose in life;

To help people make their lives easier.

It sounded so simple when the words came out of my mouth but that clarity has catapulted my business forward.

Previously I'd thought I was just here to help people but it was much more specific than that. I was determined to make things *easier* for people. After all, I'd already done all the hard work, why not use that to help others avoid making the same mistakes!

Judy and I have worked together for nearly 2 years since and I wouldn't know where to start in finding the words to thank her for everything she's done.

Then came my business mentors, James Nicholson and Jessen James.

James is a technical expert on digital marketing, which obviously made my eyes light up with excitement, and Jessen is a business strategist with the incredible ability to find exactly what's not working in any business and fix it.

Together they were such a powerful duo, Jessen would help me strategise and James would help me make it happen.

I've lost count of the amount of changes that I made in my business since working with them, even within the first week of meeting them things changed drastically.

I increased my prices by over 3 times.

I connected with higher quality clients.
I acknowledged that I was no longer a one-woman band and I started building my team.

This was where my growth really began to accelerate.

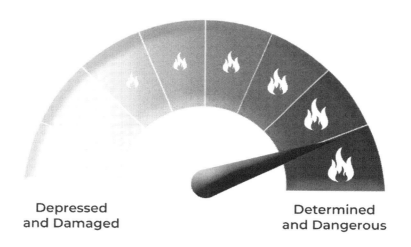

Depressed
and Damaged

Determined
and Dangerous

SECTION NINE

LIVING THE DREAM

"I'm tough, I'm ambitious, and I know exactly what I want. If that makes me a bitch, OK."

— **Madonna**

44

THINGS PEOPLE DON'T TELL YOU

Let's be honest. Running your own business is an incredible achievement and has some amazing benefits, like being able to take time off to watch your kid's sports days or work on your own schedule.

But as amazing as it can be, it's definitely not all sunshine and roses. After all, if it was easy, everyone would be doing it – right?

What people often don't talk about is what it's really like, the truth behind running your own business.

Like the fact that you'll be playing all roles in your business.

Yes, you'll have free reign over what you spend your time on and you'll be your own boss, but you'll also be everything else too, at least at the beginning.

You'll be the CEO, the business development manager, the book keeper, the digital marketer, the IT team and even the cleaner, especially if you work from home.

There were times where I had to switch roles every 30 minutes depending on what came up next on my to do list.

Customers will not find you, you must find them.

When you first start out, you'll be so excited and feel like everyone else will be just as excited and dying to work with you, but unfortunately that's not always the case.

It can be a full time job at first to get your message heard far and wide and as loud as possible so that you increase your chances of getting clients.

I had to have two interviews, a couple of networking events and a lot of Facebook posts to start generating interest in my business. After all, people can't buy if they don't know what you're selling.

There's no such thing as time off.

You might tell your clients there is, but you'll never really switch off, not at first at least.

There'll be times when you'll be awake all night, visualising new strategies you can implement.

In the corporate world, I thought working lunches were exhausting but now I had working breakfasts, lunches and dinners.

You don't always get to pick who you want to work with.

At the beginning, it's about keeping your business going and building your empire, which means you can't be fussy.

A number of times I had to work with people that I didn't really want to but it helped me really hone in on exactly who I wanted to work with.

Perfection is a myth

The most important thing that no one seems to tell you about running your own business is the fact that you don't have to be perfect.

People are always bragging about their successes in their businesses.

'Becoming a best-selling author'

'Launching a new product and generating 7 figures overnight'

'Becoming the UK's number one business coach'

But really, even starting your own business is a huge success.

Helping someone to fix a problem each and every day is amazing and something to celebrate.

You don't have to be perfect.

Your business doesn't have to be perfect.

It just needs to be what you need it to be at that point in your life.

It might be the vehicle that helps you get your freedom back.

It might be the hobby that helps you generate a bit more money for your piggy bank.

As long as it achieves whatever you're aiming for, that's the real success.

45

LISTENING TO THE RIGHT VOICE

When things are going well in business, the opportunities that are presented to you become greater and greater.

People start to see that you're succeeding and try to jump on the ride with you. It's like becoming the popular kid at school and suddenly everyone wants to be your friend.

As flattering as it can be, unfortunately not all opportunities are right for you.

New opportunities can sound interesting at first but when you start investing time and money in them, there can be times when you realise it's not in alignment with the direction you want to go in.

This is known as the 'shiny object syndrome' and I see this happen a lot with business owners.

Personally, I've wasted thousands of pounds and hundreds of hours because I've had shiny object syndrome.

New joint ventures.

New products.

New tools.

You name it, I've been distracted by it.

All I can say is that it's a good thing I take action quickly because I bounce back even quicker.

I'm not saying that all new opportunities are bad but it's about being focused enough to know which opportunities to jump into and which to walk away from.

This sounds great in principle but how does this actually happen in the real world?

Use your intuition.

I know, I know, it sounds very fluffy and that's normally not my cup of tea but hear me out.

This concept was introduced to me by a good friend of mine, Victoria Dioh.

She's a truly gifted woman with a number of businesses on the go and when I asked her how she did it she told me a huge part of her strength was in her intuition.

I was curious.

"You're telling me that I've had this superpower inside me all along that will make my life easier? Where do I sign up?"

I joke but it was a huge insight for me because often the bigger your business gets, the bigger the fear of failure. The higher the climb the harder the fall, as they say.

Victoria introduced me to the world of super-consciousness and the Super Genius family with Ryan Pinnick.

For someone like me who always likes to act first and think later, I learnt a lot from this approach.

I learnt that there are always two voices in your head:

Your intuition; and

Your ego

Your intuition is there to guide you and push you to be the best version of yourself.

Your ego is there to protect you and ensure your safety. They both have a specific purpose but the power comes in knowing which voice to listen to in different situations.

When it comes to your business, your intuition has the key to your success. The reason why a lot of businesses have a big success and then an even bigger failure is because in listening to their intuition they've achieved incredible results but as a result, they've got scared, listened to their ego and let it take over.

Ryan taught me to take away the pressure of constantly thinking about my "big vision" and just focus on the now by asking myself a simple question:

What do I want to create?

It sounds incredibly easy but it's literally that simple.

Even if you don't know the answer, just open your mouth and start talking.

"What I want to create is…" and let your intuition kick in.

The other powerful technique with super-consciousness is helping you get clarity about a challenge or a problem.

Simply think of the situation and ask yourself the question:

What is obvious?

Then start answering the question.

"What is obvious to me is…" and let your intuition kick in.

If you're anything like me, you'll feel like a right idiot the first time you do it but just trust yourself.

Your intuition will always have your back.

You just need to tune into it, like a radio.

My intuition will always be determined because that's who I am.

As soon as you learn how to turn down the volume of your ego and turn up the volume of your intuition there's literally no stopping you.

46

BUILDING MY DREAM

So, another six months on and a lot had changed.

I was no longer worrying where the next client was going to come from, I was working out how I would be able to fit everyone in!

I couldn't take on any more one to one clients because my schedule was already too full but I didn't want to turn people away that needed help.

I needed to make sure I had something that could help them even if they didn't have much money to spend.

I was offering multiple training courses on how to set up and succeed in business.

I was running weekly live training sessions to teach people how to sell online, launch new products and create social media content.

I introduced Done-For-You services for people who didn't want to learn but just wanted it all done for them.

I'd even built a team of 5 women working across the globe from Asia, Australia and UK.

I'd been running my business for over 2 years but it never really hit me how real it was, until now.

One day, I was at an event helping someone with one of their email campaigns and this guy turned to me and said "You're The Automation Queen."

The nickname travelled across a few groups and training sessions and before I knew it, it had stuck!

I was officially becoming "known".

But I had a strange realisation.

I realised I'd spent months helping other entrepreneurs package their genius through my courses but I didn't have a way for people to access EVERYTHING I had created.

I mean I had lots of individual courses, videos and templates but nowhere that had it all – one all-mighty platform.

I was constantly telling people the importance of having a strong support network and community around you without having one to offer them.

As with anything I did in business, once I had an idea, it didn't take long to make it happen.

Within two weeks, I had built a membership platform with my best videos and teachings from starting your business to building your first sales funnel and it didn't stop there.

We launched the first course in August 2018 and within the first few weeks we had 50 members!

We were having live training sessions to build their online courses, accountability groups to keep them taking action and I was sharing all of the documents and templates that I'd created over the past 2 years.

Clients were learning how to create new products, grow their social media easily and generate more sales, supporting each other throughout the whole process.

The feedback was incredible and I was absolutely loving it.

Having a cost effective way to help hundreds of people without charging a fortune, it resonated with me on a whole new level.

Over the past two years, I'd had a lot of ups and downs and made a lot of mistakes along the way and I wanted to share it so that, in the future, others didn't make the same mistakes.

So, my dream became a reality.

47

THAT MOMENT

If you've ever been involved in goal setting before, coaches often ask you to think about "What would your life be like when you've achieved that goal? How will you know?".

I'd always struggled with this part.

I was never able say how I would know when my goal had been met because it wasn't as simple as quoting a figure in my bank account, it was about much more than that.

That continued for years until one day it happened.

I knew I'd achieved my goal.

I had been working on sharing my message with more women and I'd been talking on a lot of stages at lots of different events.

I was checking my emails on the train coming back from one of the events when I saw a new email:

"Hi Chloë, here's the first draft of the cover for your review"

I opened the attachment and it was a photo of me on the cover of Global Woman magazine.

I'm not sure if I was just exhausted from being on the go but I found myself speechless.

"That's me. I'm on the cover of Global Woman magazine."

I was in shock.

It was like a dream come true.

48

THE INNER WARRIOR

Even though I had succeeded in my business, helping thousands of women, I didn't feel any different and I certainly didn't feel good enough to be on the cover of a global magazine.

But over the next few weeks I was asked to be an expert on panels for different forums and groups, I was asked to be featured on the up and coming Never Work Again Movie and it all felt like I was going to wake up and realise it was all a dream.

But it doesn't really matter how "big" you get in someone else's eyes, you'll always look the same in your own eyes.

The person staring back at you in the mirror doesn't change.

I'm still the same person that caught my boyfriend cheating, lost my job, lost my home and suffered with clinic depression but I'm also the person that's been on the cover of Global Woman magazine, met some of my biggest idols face to face and helped thousands of women all over the world.

Your wounds are what make you who you are and it might have taken over 5 years of ups and downs but I realised that both are required for true success.

From everything I'd been through, I knew that there was a warrior inside of me but she didn't need to always be ready for battle.

She was a part of me.

She still is a part of me.

The part that keeps me determined when times get hard and dangerous when times get harder.

But I've learnt when to let my guard down, be open to new experiences and let the inner warrior rest.

Deep down I know if things get tough again, she'll be back to give me the strength once more and help me get to where I need to be.

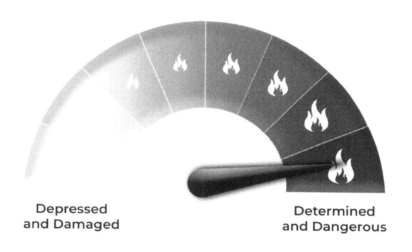

Depressed
and Damaged

Determined
and Dangerous

CONCLUSION

My friends and family have called me determined since I was a baby.

Determined to keep my Mum awake all night even though I'd been fed and changed.

Determined to get good grades at school even though I didn't fit the mould.

Determined to get a job at one of the largest accountancy firms in the world even though I didn't go to university.

Determined to set up a successful business even though I had suffered with a mental illness.

The thing that kept me going was that each time I was knocked down, I ended up reaching an even higher level.

It's like I had something more to prove and use whatever negative thing that happened to me to fuel me further and achieve even more.

Each and every time I've been knocked down, it's fuelled me to reach higher.

I've achieved way more now than I ever would have if I had never been cheated on, never had depression, never lost my job and everything else that happened along the way.

If I'd never had those experiences, I wouldn't have been fuelled to do more with my life.

I would never have found this new level of determination to do whatever I can to help people.

I hope that you've enjoyed reading this book as much as I've enjoyed writing it. I've spent years journaling my story, all of the ups and the downs, because from the minute I overcame my depression I knew I wanted to share my journey so it would help others in the future.

That's exactly what this book is all about. It's not all about me; I've shared my strategies, steps, tips and tools to help you on your journey too.

But no matter how much I've managed to squeeze into this book, there is so much more I wish I could have shared with you and so I'd love to invite you to join me in The Automation Queen Academy.

As a member of The Academy you'll receive unlimited access to all of the courses I've ever created with over 50 videos and over 100 toolkits, templates and scripts. You'll have everything you need to start your own business, build your client base and automate everything start to finish.

You will also be invited to join our monthly live calls with our amazing community of determined women who are also on their path to create their dream life. Join us at www.TheAutomationQueenAcademy.com.

Unfortunately, life is never a simple road and in this book I've shared with you the challenges I've faced. However, if you spend any time inside our communities, you'll know that there are many more challenges that women face on a daily basis, some of which you might be facing right now and you don't have to face them alone.

I want to invite you to connect with me and the other amazing people in my world. Spend time in our community Facebook group, watch our videos, come to our online events and make friends with other people like you. They may be facing totally different challenges or setting up a completely different business to yours but they have the same mission. They're striving for more and dream of creating more in their lives, for themselves and for their families.

That's what has inspired me to write this book. For you; the ladies that might read this and feel determined again to live the life that you deserve, for them; every single person that has helped me on my journey, and for me.

Words can truly set you free and sharing my journey with you has been an incredibly liberating experience.

When I hear that my story has helped others around the world it makes me feel like all of the pain was worth it.

Thank you for spending this time with me.

I'll talk to you soon!
Chloë

References

Kübler-Ross, E and Kessler, D (2005). *On Grief and Grieving: Finding the Meaning of Grief Through the Five Stages of Loss.* London, GB: Simon & Schuster

World Health Organisation. (2018). *Depression – Key Facts.* Retrieved from https://www.who.int/mental_health/management/depression/en/

Harvest Health Publishing. (2017). *What causes depression?* Retrieved from https://www.health.harvard.edu/mind-and-mood/what-causes-depression

Haig. M. (2015). *Reasons To Stay Alive.* Edinburgh, GB: Canongate Books

Maslow. A. H. (2013). *A Theory of Human Motivation.* United States of America, USA: Wilder Publications

Social Anxiety Institute. (n.d.). *What is Social Anxiety?* Retrieved from https://socialanxietyinstitute.org/what-is-social-anxiety

Bridges To Recovery. (n.d.). *High-Functioning Anxiety and Depression.* Retrieved from https://www.bridgestorecovery.com/high-functioning-anxiety/high-functioning-anxiety-depression/

Durayappah, A. (2011). *5 Scientific Reasons Why Breakups Are Devastating*. HuffPost. Retrieved from
https://www.huffpost.com/entry/breakups_b_825613

International Coaching Federation. (n.d.). *About ICF*. Retrieved from https://coachfederation.org/about

BusinessDictionary (n.d.). *Counselling*. Retrieved from
http://www.businessdictionary.com/definition/consulting.html

Management Mentors (n.d.) *Definition of Mentoring, Benefits of Mentoring, & Other FAQs*. Retrieved from
https://www.management-mentors.com/resources/corporate-mentoring-programs-resources-faqs#Q1

Bailiwick Express (n.d.). *The number of anti-depressants prescribed in Jersey*. Retrieved from
https://www.bailiwickexpress.com/jsy/news/antidepressant-prescriptions-are-still-rise/

Top University (2018) *How Much Does it Cost to Study in the UK?* Retrieved from https://www.management-mentors.com/resources/corporate-mentoring-programs-resources-faqs#Q1

School of Education (n.d.) *The Future of Education Technology* Retrieved from https://soeonline.american.edu/blog/the-future-of-education-technology

Help and Resources

National Suicide Prevention Hotline (US) – 1-800 273-8255

Suicide Prevention Hotline (UK) – 08457 909090

Better Help – https://www.betterhelp.com/

Mind – www.mind.org.uk / 0300 123 3393

Mental Health America –
http://www.mentalhealthamerica.net

Printed in Great Britain
by Amazon